MAT MAN

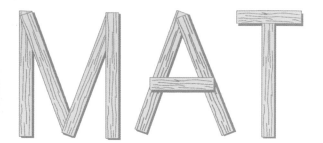
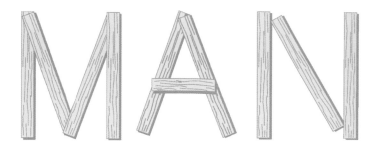

ON THE GO

By Jan Z. Olsen • Illustrations by Molly Delaney

GET SET FOR SCHOOL™

Handwriting Without Tears®
Jan Z. Olsen, OTR

8001 MacArthur Blvd
Cabin John, MD 20818
301.263.2700
www.getsetforschool.com

Printed in Hong Kong

First Edition
ISBN: 978-1-934825-39-6
3456789REGAL131211

Out the door and on his way,
what will Mat Man do today?

He'll see new things, new places too.
There is so much Mat Man can do.

At the skatepark,

Mat Man rides his skateboard.

Gliding down steep ramps with flair,

he flies on his board
through the air.

Along the path,

Mat Man pedals his bike.

The path is flat,
as flat as can be.

It's smooth for biking, with so much to see.

In the city,
Mat Man takes a taxi.

CATS

Stop and go,
Left and right,

the streets are busy
day and night.

At the zoo,

See the Giraffes!

Mat Man steps onto a bus.

His rooftop seat is up so high,
he sees a giraffe eye to eye.

At the amusement park,

Mat Man rides a rollercoaster.

The coaster ride twists in and out.

Mat Man gives
the loudest shout!

On a snowy day,
Mat Man jumps on a snowmobile.

It has no wheels, but watch it go!
It zooms so fast across the snow.

In the mountains,

Mat Man prepares his hang glider.

Soaring across the
light blue sky,

he watches birds
as they fly by.

Beside the river,
Mat Man gets ready to canoe.

It's easy to paddle with the flow.
Follow the river from high to low.

At the quarry,
Mat Man fills a dump truck.

The truck has gravel for a road.

Mat Man dumps the heavy load.

At the beach,
Mat Man rides a surfboard.

Surfers come in every size,
from little girls to great big guys.

At the port,

Mat Man boards
a tugboat.

Tugs can push and tugs can tow.
They move big ships so nice and slow.

At the air field,

Mat Man starts his biplane.

He pulls a long sign through the air.

Get Set for School!

People look.
They point and stare.

At the space center,
Mat Man is ready for launch.

Flying to the Moon or Mars,
Mat Man can explore the stars.

Home is Mat Man's favorite place
when he comes back from outer space.

Now it's time to take a rest.
Which place did you like the best?